THE
ARTISANAL
KITCHEN

SUMMER
COCKTAILS

ALSO IN THE ARTISANAL KITCHEN SERIES

Perfect Pasta

Perfect Pizza at Home

Vegetables the Italian Way

Holiday Cocktails

Holiday Cookies

Party Food

Baking for Breakfast

Party Cakes

Sweets & Treats

Barbecue Rules

Perfect Homemade Ice Cream

Gluten-Free Holiday Cookies

Jewish Holiday Baking

Barbecue Sides

THE
ARTISANAL
KITCHEN

SUMMER
COCKTAILS

Refreshing Margaritas, Mimosas, and
Daiquiris—and the World's Best Gin and Tonic

NICK MAUTONE

ARTISAN | NEW YORK

CONTENTS

INTRODUCTION

Nothing says summer like a Piña Colada (page 51) served poolside or a Mojito (page 47) in hand while flipping burgers on the grill. After all, juicy summer cocktails are the best drinks to serve with food. Their vibrant fruit flavors, crisp acidity, and thirst-quenching nature make many of these drinks ideal for summer entertaining. Furthermore, that predominance of fruit and acid is the perfect complement to almost any warm-weather meal.

The lack of formality with alfresco dining is liberating. The season's bounty offers a wealth of fruits and vegetables, making it easy for us to create fresh, inspiring food. This is no less true for cocktail making. Ripe berries and stone fruits from local farmers' markets lend their flavors to everything from fruity sangrias and refreshing cocktails to coolers and slushy frozen drinks. And that crispness is magnified in drinks like the Lime Tequila Frappé (page 37) and the Coconut Rum Frappé (page 58) with a delicious surprise: sorbet ice cubes. These easy-to-make frozen bursts of flavor transform the drinks that feature them into extra-special summertime refreshers.

No matter what you're in the mood for or what you have on hand, there's something for you here; cocktails are even arranged by base liquor, for easy browsing. If your liquor cabinet is overflowing with rum, try your hand at a Lava Flow (page 62) or the ever-popular Zombie (page 44). Or if tequila is your liquor of choice, a Frozen Raspberry Margarita (page 39) will hit the proverbial spot. If you find yourself entertaining, you can't go wrong with sparkling drinks like Champagne Sangria (page 84) or Magnificent Mimosas (page 87). And for those who don't wish to imbibe, the drink table is completed with energizing nonalcoholic beverages and not-to-be-missed virgin cocktails. From Blueberry Lemonade (page 96) to Faux Mojitos (page 100) to Virgin Watermelon Punch (page 103), there is something for everyone to enjoy this summer.

THE RIGHT TOOLS

You don't need expensive equipment to mix great drinks. There are many good affordable starter kits on the market that contain shakers, strainers, jiggers, bar spoons, and paring knives. Aside from the household basics—a bottle opener, can opener, and corkscrew—here are some other tools you will need.

SHAKERS

There are two types of cocktail shakers: the cobbler shaker and the Boston shaker. Either one works well, although each has particular features that make it useful. Specifically, the cobbler comes in varying sizes, from 8 to 16 to 24 ounces and even larger. These variations allow for different drink sizes and some flexibility when presenting and serving cocktails. For the shaking and stirring technique, see page 10.

To use a cobbler, fill the base shaker with ice and the cocktail ingredients. Put the top on with the cap in place. Shake well, remove the cap, and strain the drink into a glass.

The Boston shaker is the one most bartenders use. It is a little more versatile than the cobbler but slightly more difficult to use. The Boston is composed of two metal tumblers or one glass tumbler and one metal tumbler. One tumbler holds roughly 26 to 30 ounces. The other tumbler generally holds 16 ounces. To use a Boston, fill the smaller tumbler with the cocktail ingredients and ice. Place the larger tumbler on top and gently but firmly give it a tap or two to seal the two tumblers together. Hold the bottom of the smaller tumbler in the palm of one hand while pressing the larger tumbler with the palm of the other and shake vigorously. Invert the shaker on a counter so that the larger half is on the bottom. Hold the seal between the two pieces with one hand; two fingers should be on one end and two fingers on the other. Hold firmly and, with the heel of your other hand, tap the rim of the larger tumbler. This should break the seal. Remove the smaller tumbler carefully. Place a strainer over the top of the larger tumbler and pour.

STRAINERS

The Hawthorn strainer and the julep strainer each serve their own purpose, and both are necessary if using a Boston shaker set. The Hawthorn strainer has a metal coil on its underside, and the julep strainer is solid metal with holes throughout. The Hawthorn is used for shaken drinks and works with the larger tumbler, and the julep strainer is used for stirred drinks and is used with the smaller tumbler.

JIGGERS

Jiggers are basically tiny measuring cups. The most common jiggers have a long handle with two cups of different sizes that measure 2 ounces or less, but the best jiggers, if you can find them, are small, shot glass–size measuring cups with measurements ranging from ¼ to 1 ounce and their equivalencies in teaspoons, tablespoons, and milliliters all etched on the side.

COCKTAIL SPOONS

Cocktail spoons are used to stir a drink in a pitcher or shaker. Stir until the outside of the shaker is frosted and beaded with sweat, ten to fifteen seconds.

KNIVES

For cocktail making, you will need a paring knife for cutting your lemons, limes, and oranges and a chef's knife for cutting large fruit such as pineapples.

CHANNEL KNIVES AND ZESTERS

A channel knife has a rounded or rectangular metal head with a small curved blade and a hole on either the side or the top. This is used for producing long citrus-peel swirls. A zester has a steel edge with five tiny cutting holes. When pulled across the surface of an orange, lemon, or lime, it creates strips of peel.

MUDDLERS

Bar muddlers are used for mashing fruit, sometimes with sugar, to extract the juice. They are also used for bruising soft fruit, such as cherries, and herbs, such as mint. The best muddlers are made of soft, unvarnished wood and are generally 6 inches long with a flat end on one side.

JUICERS AND REAMERS

Make sure to get a citrus juicer model that is large enough to handle grapefruit as well as lemons and limes. In addition, always keep a wooden citrus reamer on hand. It is great if you have to juice just a few lemons or limes.

COCKTAIL PITCHERS

Tall, elongated, and somewhat narrow, cocktail pitchers range in size from 1 to 2 quarts. Standard cocktail pitchers also come with a long glass stirrer. Gallon-size glass pitchers and several plastic pitchers with tight-fitting lids are also good to have on hand.

THE RIGHT TECHNIQUES

There are very few strict rules for mixing drinks, and with just a bit of practice you can easily master them all.

SHAKING AND STIRRING

When shaking your drinks, follow this simple but important rule: shake vigorously until the outside of the shaker is frosted and beaded with sweat. The shaker should be so cold that it is almost painful to hold. This will generally take ten to fifteen seconds. Most important, maintain a consistent and constant rhythm while shaking to ensure that the drink is mixed effectively.

As for shaking versus stirring, generally, drinks that are all or mostly liquor, such as a martini, should be stirred; drinks that contain juice, egg, or other heavy ingredients should be shaken. The simple reason for this is texture: in cocktails that are primarily or all liquor, stirring produces a more delicate texture; for juice-based or weightier drinks, shaking emulsifies the cocktail, ensuring a smooth, even texture.

For very weighty drinks or those based on fruit purees, a technique called rolling is the best method for mixing and can be done only in a Boston shaker. Rolling consists of pouring a drink back and forth between the two tumblers. This thoroughly combines heavy juices with other ingredients without producing a foamy texture that is unpleasant in these types of drinks.

MUDDLING

To muddle, place the fruit, herbs, sugar, or other ingredients to be muddled in the bottom of a large glass or shaker. Using the flat end of the muddler, firmly press and twist the tool, crushing and breaking down the fruit or herb to release as much juice and essential oil as possible. If bruising an herb, do not press quite as hard; you don't want to pulverize it.

RIMMING

Rimming a glass with sugar, salt, or spices ensures that every sip of the cocktail is a multilayered experience.

The key to proper rimming is to keep the granules on the *outside* of the glass. Too many granules on the inside of the rim mean that each time the drinker tips their glass, the garnish falls into the cocktail, eventually throwing off the balance of flavors in the whole drink. The *correct* method is to pour the sugar or salt onto a small plate, rub the juicy side of a wedge of lemon, lime, or other citrus fruit on the *outer* edge of the rim—not along the inside—and holding the glass at an angle, roll the outer edge of the rim in the salt or sugar until it is fully coated.

FLOATING

Floating is a technique that has both aesthetic and practical benefits. Brightly colored syrups, cordials, or cream may be floated on a cocktail, giving an attractive layered look to the drink and dividing the drink into two distinct levels in the drinker's mouth. To float one liquid on top of the other, place the bowl of a spoon upside down over the cocktail and pour the cream or syrup slowly over it, allowing the liquid to gently spread over the top of the drink.

GIN

GIN IS A distillate of cereal grains, especially corn and barley, although wheat and rye are also used. It is distilled three times (rectified), and during the distillation process, aromatic herbs and spices called botanicals are infused into the base neutral spirit. All gin includes juniper, and most gins contain six to ten different botanicals (like coriander, angelica, orange peel, and cardamom).

THE TWO MOST prominent styles of gin are Dutch and London dry. Dutch gin is 70 to 80 proof (35 to 40 percent alcohol) and is made from rye, corn, and barley and distilled in pot stills and aged in oak casks. This gin is excellent on its own or as a mixer. London dry gin is higher in alcohol than Dutch gin. The botanicals are added during the distillation process when the base spirit is actually in a vapor form before recondensing. This is a perfect martini gin or great as a mixer.

SINGAPORE SLING

If you look up this recipe in a hundred different cocktail books, you'll get a hundred different versions. Some recipes call for the addition of ½ ounce Bénédictine (an aromatic French cordial) or ½ ounce Cointreau to each serving for sweetness and complexity. Others call for a dash of pineapple juice or bitters. There are even some that call for all of the above.

ICE FOR SERVING

8 OUNCES GIN

2 OUNCES CHERRY HEERING (SEE STRAIGHT UP) OR CHERRY BRANDY

2 OUNCES FRESH LEMON JUICE (FROM APPROXIMATELY 2 LEMONS)

2 OUNCES SIMPLE SYRUP, PINEAPPLE SYRUP, OR GINGER SYRUP (RECIPES FOLLOW)

16 OUNCES CLUB SODA

4 ORANGE SLICES FOR GARNISH

4 MARASCHINO CHERRIES, HOMEMADE (RECIPE FOLLOWS) OR STORE-BOUGHT, FOR GARNISH

GLASSWARE

4 HIGHBALL GLASSES

Fill the highball glasses with ice.

Fill a cocktail shaker with ice and add the gin, Cherry Heering, lemon juice, and syrup. Shake vigorously until the outside of the shaker is thoroughly beaded with sweat and is extremely cold to the touch.

Strain into the glasses and top each with 4 ounces club soda. Garnish each with an orange slice and a cherry and serve.

STRAIGHT UP
Cherry Heering is a Danish cherry liqueur invented in the late nineteenth century. It is easy to find and quite delicious. If you cannot find Cherry Heering, use cherry brandy instead.

MARASCHINO CHERRIES

This homemade version of the traditional "cocktail cherry" requires very little effort. Though it is used sparingly, the grape juice adds body and complexity to the syrup, enhancing the flavor and color of the cherries and balancing out any unripe undertones. The star anise adds a hint of the exotic; if it's unavailable, cardamom or cinnamon can be used instead. Almond, a traditional pairing with cherry, adds a mellow roundness to the cherries. The melding of these flavors happens during the long steeping in the refrigerator. During the winter when fresh cherries are not available, substitute frozen cherries.

1½ CUPS WATER

½ CUP RED GRAPE JUICE (USE 100% JUICE)

1 CUP SUGAR

3½ OUNCES FRESH LEMON JUICE
(FROM APPROXIMATELY 3 LEMONS)

PINCH OF SALT

1 WHOLE PIECE OF STAR ANISE

1 POUND SWEET CHERRIES, PITTED

1 TEASPOON ALMOND EXTRACT

PLANNING AHEAD
The cherries can be made up to 2 weeks in advance and stored in the refrigerator. The cherries are ready as soon as they are cool but are better if steeped at least 24 hours.

Combine the water, grape juice, sugar, lemon juice, salt, and star anise in a nonreactive saucepan and bring to a boil over medium-high heat. Reduce the heat and simmer the mixture until the sugar has dissolved, approximately 5 minutes.

Add the cherries and almond extract. Simmer on low heat for 10 minutes or until the cherries have exuded some of their juice and the syrup has taken on a distinctly cherry flavor. Be careful not to overcook. The point is not to actually cook the cherries but to heat them in the syrup just long enough to bring out their essence.

Remove the pan from the heat, transfer the cherries and the syrup to a bowl, and let cool to room temperature. Transfer to a container with a tight-fitting lid, cover tightly, and refrigerate. The longer the cherries steep, the more flavorful they will become.

VARIATION

Quick Maraschinos: When fresh cherries are at their ripest and juiciest during the summer, you can easily prepare quick homemade maraschinos. Sprinkle a handful of pitted cherries with a teaspoon or two of sugar, stir, and refrigerate for 1 hour before using.

SIMPLE SYRUP

MAKES 2 CUPS SYRUP

This recipe for plain sugar syrup provides the base for most of the syrup recipes that follow. For a lighter syrup, omit 1 cup of sugar and proceed as directed.

2 CUPS SUGAR

1 CUP WATER

PLANNING AHEAD
The syrup can be made up to 2 weeks in advance and stored in a very clean container in the refrigerator.

Place the sugar and water in a small saucepan and stir to combine. Bring to a gentle boil over medium-high heat. Reduce the heat and simmer until the sugar is completely dissolved and the syrup is slightly thickened, about 3 minutes.

(continued)

Remove from the heat and let cool. Transfer the syrup to a container with a tight-fitting lid, cover, and refrigerate until ready to use.

VARIATIONS
....

Berry Syrup: This variation can be made up to 1 week in advance and yields 2¼ cups syrup. After bringing the sugar and water mixture to a gentle boil, add 1 pint berries, rinsed and stemmed, and reduce the heat. Simmer until the syrup has taken on the color and aroma of the berries, about 10 minutes. Once the syrup has cooled, strain it through a fine-mesh strainer, pressing the berries to extract their juice, and store as directed above.

Ginger Syrup: Add one 3-inch length of gingerroot, peeled and cut into six ½-inch pieces, and 2 tablespoons fresh lime juice (from approximately 1 lime) to the sugar and water mixture. After removing from the heat, discard the ginger pieces and store as directed above.

Mint Syrup: Add 1 bunch mint, approximately 3 ounces, rinsed, with roots trimmed, to the sugar and water mixture. Simmer for 5 minutes instead of 3. When the syrup has cooled, remove the mint and store as directed at left.

Pineapple Syrup: This variation can be made up to 1 week in advance and yields 3½ cups syrup. Cut a small pineapple into 1-inch chunks and add it to 3 cups sugar and 1½ cups water. Simmer for 15 minutes instead of 3, until the pineapple has a glossy, candied look and has exuded its juice. Once the syrup has cooled, strain out the pineapple and store as directed at left.

Vanilla Syrup: After combining the sugar and water, split a vanilla bean in half lengthwise. With the back of a small knife, scrape out the seeds and add the seeds and the bean halves to the saucepan. After removing from the heat, let the syrup cool, remove the vanilla bean halves, and store as directed at left.

PINEAPPLE SLING

This drink demonstrates perfectly how a well-balanced classic, in this case the Singapore Sling (page 15), lends itself to improvisation. Switch one liquor for another and tweak just slightly the supporting ingredients, and you have a new distinct, mouthwatering drink. In this one, the combination of pineapple and gin is delicious. If you have time, try soaking the pineapple wedges in the gin—for as little as 10 minutes and up to an hour—for extra flavor.

ICE FOR SERVING

8 OUNCES GIN

2 OUNCES CHERRY HEERING (SEE STRAIGHT UP, PAGE 15) OR CHERRY BRANDY

3 OUNCES FRESH LEMON JUICE (FROM APPROXIMATELY 2 LEMONS)

2 OUNCES PINEAPPLE SYRUP (PAGE 18)

16 OUNCES CLUB SODA

4 PINEAPPLE WEDGES FOR GARNISH

4 MARASCHINO CHERRIES, HOMEMADE (SEE PAGE 16) OR STORE-BOUGHT, FOR GARNISH

GLASSWARE

4 HIGHBALL GLASSES

Fill the highball glasses with ice.

Fill a cocktail shaker with ice. Add the gin, Cherry Heering, lemon juice, and syrup. Shake vigorously until the outside of the shaker is thoroughly beaded with sweat and is extremely cold to the touch.

Strain into the glasses and top each with 4 ounces club soda. Garnish each with a pineapple wedge and a cherry and serve.

TOM COLLINS

The Tom Collins takes its name from the Old Tom sweetened gin originally used to make this simple cocktail such a wonderful light aperitif.

ICE FOR SERVING

8 OUNCES GIN

6 OUNCES LEMON SOUR MIX (RECIPE FOLLOWS)

16 OUNCES CLUB SODA

4 ORANGE SLICES FOR GARNISH

4 MARASCHINO CHERRIES, HOMEMADE (SEE PAGE 16) OR STORE-BOUGHT, FOR GARNISH

GLASSWARE

4 COLLINS GLASSES

Fill the collins glasses with ice.

Fill a cocktail shaker with ice and add the gin and sour mix. Shake vigorously until the outside of the shaker is thoroughly beaded with sweat and is extremely cold to the touch.

Strain into the glasses and top each with 4 ounces club soda. Garnish each with an orange slice and a cherry and serve.

(continued)

VARIATION
....

Rum Collins: Replace the gin with dark rum.

LEMON OR LIME SOUR MIX

Egg whites, which help emulsify the ingredients, are traditional in sour mix. Raw egg has the potential to carry foodborne illness, so enjoy with caution (or use powdered pasteurized egg whites). This recipe halves or doubles perfectly.

24 TO 30 LEMONS OR LIMES

I CUP EGG WHITES, FROM APPROXIMATELY 8 LARGE EGGS OR 6 TO 7 JUMBO EGGS

I CUP SIMPLE SYRUP (PAGE 17), OR MORE TO TASTE

PLANNING AHEAD

This mix can be prepared in advance and refrigerated for several days or frozen for several weeks. For longer-term storage, you can juice all the fruit in advance and freeze the juice in a tightly sealed container for up to 1 month. Transfer it to the refrigerator to defrost at least 24 hours before using.

Juice the fruit and pour the juice through a fine-mesh strainer into a bowl. Using a rubber spatula, scrape the pulp through the strainer to ensure that you get every drop of juice. Discard the pulp. You should have 1 quart of juice, which generally requires 24 to 30 lemons or limes. Use more if needed.

Add the egg whites and syrup and whisk thoroughly.

Strain the mixture once more through a fine-mesh strainer into a container with a tight-fitting lid. Sample the mix. It should taste true to the fruit but with a hint of sweetness. If you prefer it sweeter, add more syrup. Depending on the time of year, the acid and sugar in the lemons and limes can vary, so adjust the syrup as needed.

Cover and chill thoroughly before using.

TRICK OF THE TRADE

Try replacing the simple syrup in sour mix with any of the flavored syrups. For example, use Pineapple Syrup (page 18) in the lime sour mix for a more tropical style, or use Vanilla Syrup (page 18) in the lemon sour mix to give it a mellow yet exotic flavor.

GIN RICKEY

Created in the late 1800s by a bartender at Shoomaker's bar in Washington, DC, the gin rickey is named after Democratic lobbyist Colonel Joseph Rickey. The addition of citrus and soda to gin makes this an extremely refreshing cocktail.

ICE FOR SERVING

8 OUNCES GIN

2 OUNCES FRESH LIME JUICE (FROM APPROXIMATELY 2 LARGE LIMES)

20 OUNCES CLUB SODA

4 LIME WEDGES FOR GARNISH

GLASSWARE

4 HIGHBALL GLASSES

Fill the highball glasses with ice.

Fill a cocktail shaker with ice and add the gin and lime juice. Shake vigorously until the outside of the shaker is thoroughly beaded with sweat and is extremely cold to the touch.

Divide the cocktail among the glasses. Top each with club soda, garnish with a lime wedge, and serve.

VARIATIONS

Orange Rickey: Replace 2 ounces of the gin with 2 ounces Cointreau to give a hint of sweetness.

Pineapple Rickey: Add 4 ounces Pineapple Syrup (page 18) for a tropical touch.

Rum Rickey: Replace the gin with rum.

GIN-GER & TONIC

The Gin-ger & Tonic is best in the summer months, when the temperature is high and guests need to slake their thirst. It is a perfect barbecue cocktail, enhancing the smoky and salty flavors of the grill with its combination of sweet tang and mild bitterness. It also stands well on its own at a cocktail party, since it is neither too sweet nor too tart and can therefore go with almost any type of hors d'oeuvre. It is very easy to adapt this recipe for either a smaller or bigger crowd.

8 OUNCES GINGER SYRUP (PAGE 18)

1 LITER TANQUERAY NO. TEN GIN OR ANOTHER DRY GIN

ONE 1- TO 1½-INCH LENGTH OF GINGER, PEELED AND HALVED

2 LIMES, CUT INTO WEDGES

ICE FOR SERVING

ABOUT 2 LITERS TONIC WATER

2 LIMES, EACH CUT CROSSWISE INTO 5 ROUNDS, FOR GARNISH

GLASSWARE

10 LARGE WINEGLASSES

PLANNING AHEAD
The cocktail mix requires at least 24 hours in the refrigerator and will keep for 1 month. (Remove the ginger and lime wedges after 24 hours.)

Pour the ginger syrup into a 2-quart canning jar or other container with a tight-fitting lid and add the gin, ginger, and lime wedges. Stir, cover, and refrigerate for at least 24 hours. Remove the ginger and lime wedges after 24 hours.

To serve, fill the wineglasses with ice. Divide the gin mixture among the glasses (each should be about half full) and top off with tonic water. Float a fresh lime slice on each cocktail and serve.

CITRUS GIN

This is a particular favorite in the hottest months—a gin martini with a summery edge. Angostura bitters can be used in place of the orange bitters; they will change the color of the drink from yellow to pink.

4 OUNCES GIN

I OUNCE DRY VERMOUTH

I OUNCE LIMONCELLO, HOMEMADE (RECIPE FOLLOWS) OR STORE-BOUGHT

4 DASHES ORANGE BITTERS

GLASSWARE
2 COCKTAIL GLASSES

Fill a cocktail pitcher with ice and add the gin, vermouth, limoncello, and bitters. Stir vigorously until the outside of the pitcher is beaded with sweat and frosty.

Strain into the cocktail glasses and serve.

LIMONCELLO

Limoncello's vibrant lemon flavor, subtle sweetness, good acidity, and hint of bitterness make it an incredible digestif as well as a perfect mixer with other liquors and juices. You can also make this with oranges, limes, and even clementines. Keep a bottle on hand in the freezer, where it will remain liquid but slushy.

12 LEMONS

1½ CUPS SUGAR, OR MORE TO TASTE

ONE 1-LITER BOTTLE VODKA OR GRAPPA

PLANNING AHEAD
The maceration requires 7 days in the refrigerator. The limoncello can be stored indefinitely in the freezer.

Juice the lemons and reserve the juice for another purpose. Cut the remaining rind into quarters.

Place the lemon rind and sugar in a large pitcher with a tight-fitting lid and stir well, using a spoon to break up the lemons to help extract any remaining juice.

Add the vodka or grappa (save the bottle for storing the limoncello later) and stir well.

Cover and refrigerate for 24 hours, then stir well and taste, adding more sugar if necessary.

Refrigerate for 6 days more, stirring every day.

Strain the mixture through a fine-mesh strainer, pressing the lemons against the sides of the strainer to extract all the limoncello. Pour into the reserved spirit bottle and store in the freezer.

SUMMER BUCK

Bucks are basically gin and ginger ale with lots of fruit added. This version uses ripe mangoes, but you can use papaya, any melon, or citrus fruit instead.

I SMALL RIPE MANGO

ICE FOR SERVING

4 DASHES ANGOSTURA BITTERS

I LEMON, QUARTERED

8 OUNCES GIN

16 OUNCES GINGER ALE

GLASSWARE

4 HIGHBALL GLASSES

Peel the mango and cut the flesh into ½-inch cubes, discarding the hard pit.

Fill each highball glass halfway with ice. Spoon a generous amount of mango into each glass, then fill the rest of the way with ice.

Add a dash of bitters to each glass. Squeeze a lemon wedge into each, then drop the wedge into the glass.

Pour 2 ounces gin and 4 ounces ginger ale into each glass and serve.

TEQUILA

TEQUILA, AN INTERESTING, delicious spirit, is made from the heart, or piña, of the blue agave cactus. Mexican law very strictly regulates the different categories of tequila, the main two of which are mixto and 100 percent agave. Mixto, as its name implies, is a mix: 51 percent agave mash and up to 49 percent other sugars, such as cane or beet; 100 percent agave is distilled solely from the blue agave plant. Within both mixto and 100 percent agave, there are four main subcategories: blanco, joven abocado, reposado, and añejo. Blanco, white, silver, and plata all mean the same thing: tequila that is aged fewer than sixty days in wood. Joven abocado is also known as gold tequila. The color comes from other flavoring and coloring agents. Reposado means "rested" in Spanish. These tequilas must age at least sixty days in wood, and many are aged at least a year; they can also have flavoring and coloring agents. Añejo means "aged," and by law it must spend at least a year in wood, though most actually spend a longer time. One hundred percent agave añejo is a fantastic tequila. It has pronounced complex and earth notes, and while it has a bite, the extra aging in wood mellows the sharp or bitter tones.

MARGARITA

The margarita is among the most popular drinks ever. One reason for the demand is that its balanced blend of sweet-tart earthiness and acidity cuts through the richness and spice of many foods.

KOSHER SALT FOR RIMMING THE GLASSES

4 OUNCES FRESH LIME JUICE (FROM APPROXIMATELY 4 LIMES), SOME LIME RIND RESERVED FOR RIMMING THE GLASSES

8 OUNCES TEQUILA

6 OUNCES COINTREAU

4 LIME ROUNDS FOR GARNISH

GLASSWARE

4 MARGARITA COUPES OR COCKTAIL GLASSES

Pour the salt onto a small plate. Cut the reserved lime rind as necessary and rub the juicy side along the outer edge of the lip of each coupe—not along the inside of the rim. Holding each coupe at an angle, roll the outer edge of the rim in the salt until it is fully coated.

Fill a cocktail shaker with ice and add the lime juice, tequila, and Cointreau. Shake vigorously until the outside of the shaker is beaded with sweat and frosty.

Strain into the prepared coupes, garnish with lime rounds, and serve.

(continued)

Frothy Margarita: Substitute 4 ounces Lime Sour Mix (page 22) for the lime juice.

Frozen Margarita: Place the tequila, Cointreau, and lime juice in a large pitcher without ice and stir to mix. Process in a blender in batches, using 1 cup crushed ice and 4½ ounces mix per serving. Blend until smooth and pour into salted coupes.

Grand Margarita: Replace the Cointreau with Grand Marnier, which has a much more pronounced orange flavor and more intensity. Garnish with orange zest.

LIME TEQUILA FRAPPÉ

For this cocktail, use a silver tequila such as Chinaco Blanco, which has a clean flavor with a great backbite and yet is still earthy, the way tequila should be. Gold and añejo tequilas tend to dominate too much in this drink.

1 PINT LIME SORBET

8 FRESH MINT SPRIGS

2 TEASPOONS SUGAR

8 OUNCES SILVER TEQUILA

CRUSHED ICE FOR SERVING

8 OUNCES CLUB SODA

GLASSWARE

4 OLD-FASHIONED GLASSES

PLANNING AHEAD
The sorbet ice cubes should be made at least 1 hour before serving and can be made up to a week in advance and stored in the freezer.

To prepare the sorbet ice cubes, let the sorbet soften at room temperature for 15 minutes or microwave it for 30 seconds. Spread the sorbet into an ice cube tray and freeze until solid, at least 1 hour.

When ready to serve, place 2 mint sprigs and ½ teaspoon sugar in each old-fashioned glass. Gently muddle together (see page 11).

Add the tequila and stir well. Add the sorbet ice cubes and enough crushed ice to fill the glasses. Top off with club soda and serve.

FROZEN RASPBERRY MARGARITA

MAKES FOUR 12-OUNCE DRINKS

The texture of raspberries and their intense flavor help make a truly great blended margarita.

8 OUNCES TEQUILA

3 OUNCES TRIPLE SEC

3 OUNCES CRÈME DE FRAMBOISE

6 OUNCES FRESH LIME JUICE (FROM APPROXIMATELY 6 LIMES), SOME RINDS RESERVED FOR RIMMING THE GLASSES

KOSHER SALT FOR RIMMING THE GLASSES

CRUSHED ICE FOR SERVING

½ PINT FRESH RASPBERRIES

GLASSWARE

4 HURRICANE GLASSES OR ANY OTHER LARGE GLASSES

PLANNING AHEAD
The base can be made up to 8 hours in advance and stored in the refrigerator.

In a cocktail pitcher, mix the tequila, triple sec, crème de framboise, and lime juice.

When ready to serve, pour the salt onto a small plate. Rub the juicy side of the reserved lime rind along the outer edge of the lip of each hurricane glass—not along the inside of the rim. Holding each glass at an angle, roll the outer edge of the rim in the salt until it is fully coated.

Blend the margarita in two batches, using 10 ounces mix, 2 cups crushed ice, and half of the raspberries for each batch. Blend until smooth.

Pour into the prepared glasses and serve.

CHAPTER

-**3**-

RUM

RUM IS MADE from molasses, sugarcane juice, or cane syrup. There are three basic kinds of rum: light-bodied, medium-bodied, and heavy-bodied. Light-bodied rum, also called white or silver, is aged for up to one year in casks and is filtered before bottling, which makes the rum fairly neutral. Medium-bodied rum, often called gold or amber, is aged in wood longer than light rum and often has added caramel for even color. This rum is richer and smoother than light rum. Heavy-bodied rum has two distinctly different subcategories: blended rums and well-aged sipping rums. Blended rums are dark and heavily colored and have a distinct weight in the mouth. The well-aged sipping rums are kept in casks much longer than all other rums and take on a brandy-like flavor; they can be sipped on their own or mixed in drinks. Rum is produced all over the Caribbean and West Indies, with each island making its own distinctive rums. Have some fun and treat yourself to an island comparison.

CLASSIC DAIQUIRI

MAKES FOUR 3½-OUNCE DRINKS

The daiquiri was created in Cuba and named after the town of the same name. Its beauty is in its simplicity: rum, lime, and sugar come together in a succulent and refreshing beverage. The daiquiri took off after it was discovered by Ernest Hemingway, whose favorite variation was called the Papa Doble and included a few drops of maraschino liqueur and a dash of grapefruit juice.

8 OUNCES LIGHT RUM

8 OUNCES LIME SOUR MIX (PAGE 22)

4 THIN, ROUND LIME SLICES FOR GARNISH

GLASSWARE

4 COCKTAIL GLASSES

Fill a cocktail shaker with ice and add the rum and sour mix. Shake vigorously until the shaker is beaded with sweat and frosty and the mixture is frothy.

Strain into the cocktail glasses, float a lime slice on top of each, and serve.

ZOMBIE

Depending on whom you ask, the creation of the zombie is alternately credited to Trader Vic, the legendary restaurateur, and Don the Beachcomber, another restaurateur who traveled the beaches of the world. Either way, the zombie is the perfect drink to kick off a summer barbecue.

10 OUNCES FRESH ORANGE JUICE
(FROM APPROXIMATELY 3 ORANGES)

4 OUNCES FRESH LEMON JUICE
(FROM APPROXIMATELY 3 LEMONS)

4 OUNCES FRESH LIME JUICE
(FROM APPROXIMATELY 4 LIMES)

6 OUNCES APRICOT BRANDY

6 OUNCES DARK RUM

6 OUNCES LIGHT RUM

2 OUNCES GRENADINE, HOMEMADE
(RECIPE FOLLOWS) OR STORE-BOUGHT

½ OUNCE ANGOSTURA BITTERS

CRUSHED ICE FOR SERVING

FRESH MINT LEAVES FOR GARNISH

6 PINEAPPLE WEDGES FOR GARNISH

GLASSWARE

6 HURRICANE GLASSES
OR COOLER GLASSES

Fill a large pitcher with ice and add the citrus juices, apricot brandy, dark rum, light rum, grenadine, and bitters. Stir briskly until the pitcher is beaded with sweat and frosty.

Fill the hurricane glasses with crushed ice and strain the cocktail over the ice.

Garnish each glass with several mint leaves and a pineapple wedge and serve.

VARIATION

Zombie Punch: Double the recipe and serve in a punch bowl; this yields approximately twenty-four 4-ounce punch cup servings.

GRENADINE

True grenadine syrup is made from pomegranate juice. It is used as a sweetener and coloring agent for many cocktails and punches, perhaps most famously lending its red hue to the Shirley Temple and the tequila sunrise. Unfortunately, most of the grenadine on the market is made from corn syrup and artificial coloring. With a little searching, you can find a real version, but making your own is quick and easy. This grenadine is a clear red color but not as intense as the artificially colored versions. If you want deep red grenadine, substitute 1 cup cranberry juice for 1 cup of the water.

6 POMEGRANATES

2 CUPS SUGAR

2 CUPS WATER

PLANNING AHEAD

The grenadine can be made up to 2 weeks in advance and stored in a very clean container in the refrigerator.

Cut the pomegranates into quarters and remove the fruit with a paring knife, discarding the skin. Place the fruit in a medium saucepan with the sugar. Muddle the two together (see page 11) to extract the juice from the pomegranate.

Stir in the water and bring to a gentle boil over medium-high heat. Reduce the heat and simmer, stirring regularly, for about 10 minutes.

Remove from the heat and let cool. Strain the syrup into a container with a tight-fitting lid; discard the fruit. Cover and refrigerate until ready to use.

TRICK OF THE TRADE

Store the syrup in a squeeze bottle so you can quickly add a "float" (see page 11) to the Lava Flow (page 62).

MOJITO

The mojito was the original drink of the Cuban working class. A cooling, thirst-quenching mojito was a great way to end the day. The current formalized recipe was created at the La Bodeguita hotel in Cuba, one of Hemingway's haunts. If you prefer this drink short and stronger, cut the seltzer to 4 ounces or omit it.

12 FRESH MINT SPRIGS

4 OUNCES SIMPLE SYRUP (PAGE 17)

4 OUNCES FRESH LIME JUICE
(FROM APPROXIMATELY 4 LIMES)

ICE FOR SERVING

8 OUNCES WHITE RUM

24 OUNCES SELTZER

GLASSWARE

4 HIGHBALL GLASSES

In each of the highball glasses, place 2 mint sprigs, 1 ounce syrup, and 1 ounce lime juice. Muddle the ingredients together (see page 11).

Add ice and 2 ounces rum to each glass and stir to blend.

Fill each glass with seltzer, garnish with the remaining mint, and serve.

FLORIDITA

This cocktail was created at the Floridita Hotel in Cuba sometime in the 1920s or '30s. The addition of the grapefruit juice gives the Floridita a bit of tang.

4 OUNCES WHITE RUM

3 OUNCES FRESH GRAPEFRUIT JUICE
(FROM APPROXIMATELY ½ GRAPEFRUIT)

2 OUNCES FRESH LIME JUICE (FROM
APPROXIMATELY 2 LIMES)

1 OUNCE TRIPLE SEC

1 OUNCE MARASCHINO LIQUEUR

1 OUNCE GRENADINE, HOMEMADE
(SEE PAGE 45) OR STORE-BOUGHT

2 FRESH MINT LEAVES FOR GARNISH

GLASSWARE
2 COCKTAIL GLASSES

Fill a cocktail shaker with ice and add the rum, grapefruit juice, lime juice, triple sec, maraschino liqueur, and grenadine. Shake vigorously until the outside of the shaker is beaded with sweat and frosty.

Strain into the cocktail glasses, garnish with mint leaves, and serve.

SWIZZLE

This drink is named after the swizzle stick. The original swizzle sticks were created in Jamaica and were twelve or more inches long with spikes on the bottom that helped mix the drink.

CRUSHED ICE FOR SERVING

4 OUNCES JAMAICAN RUM

2 OUNCES SIMPLE SYRUP (PAGE 17)

I OUNCE FRESH LIME JUICE (FROM APPROXIMATELY I LIME)

I OUNCE FRESH LEMON JUICE (FROM APPROXIMATELY I LEMON)

2 DASHES ANGOSTURA BITTERS

2 LIME WEDGES FOR GARNISH

GLASSWARE

2 HIGHBALL GLASSES

Fill the highball glasses with crushed ice.

Fill a cocktail shaker with ice and add the rum, syrup, citrus juices, and bitters. Shake vigorously until the outside of the shaker is beaded with sweat and frosty.

Strain into the glasses, garnish with lime wedges, and serve.

PIÑA COLADA

MAKES EIGHT 17-OUNCE DRINKS

Created in the 1950s at the Caribe Hilton in Puerto Rico, the piña colada evokes island paradise better than any other tropical drink. Seventeen ounces may seem like a huge drink, but remember that each cocktail has 8 ounces ice and only $2\frac{1}{2}$ ounces rum. Replace 8 ounces of the cream of coconut with heavy cream to yield a smoother, richer drink. Use spiced rum instead of the Myers's rum for a little more complexity. Note that you will need a blender to make this drink.

32 OUNCES PINEAPPLE JUICE

24 OUNCES COCO LOPEZ CREAM OF COCONUT OR 16 OUNCES COCO LOPEZ CREAM OF COCONUT AND 8 OUNCES HEAVY CREAM

12 OUNCES LIGHT RUM

8 OUNCES MYERS'S RUM

8 CUPS CRUSHED ICE

8 PINEAPPLE WEDGES FOR GARNISH

GLASSWARE

8 HURRICANE GLASSES OR OTHER LARGE SPECIALTY GLASSES, CHILLED

PLANNING AHEAD
Combine all but the crushed ice and the garnish up to 8 hours in advance and refrigerate it until you are ready to blend.

Mix the pineapple juice, cream of coconut, and both rums in a large pitcher. If desired, cover and refrigerate for up to 8 hours.

When ready to blend, do so in batches, using 1 cup crushed ice and 9 ounces mix per serving. Process in a blender on medium speed until smooth.

Pour into the hurricane glasses, garnish each with a pineapple wedge, and serve.

MAI TAI

MAKES TWO 4-OUNCE DRINKS

The mai tai was created by Victor Bergeron at his California restaurant, Trader Vic's, in the 1940s. Too often, mai tais are served in really large glasses and don't do justice to the original drink. When made with premium ingredients and kept to a reasonable size, this drink will live up to its name, which means "out of this world" in Tahitian. If you cannot find orgeat syrup, use amaretto in its place.

ICE FOR SERVING

4 OUNCES DARK RUM

1½ OUNCES TRIPLE SEC

1½ OUNCES FRESH LIME JUICE
(FROM 1 TO 1½ LIMES)

½ OUNCE ORGEAT SYRUP
(SEE STRAIGHT UP) OR AMARETTO

2 FRESH MINT LEAVES FOR GARNISH

2 LIME WEDGES FOR GARNISH

GLASSWARE

2 ROCKS GLASSES

Fill the rocks glasses with ice.

Fill a cocktail shaker with ice and add the rum, triple sec, lime juice, and orgeat syrup. Shake vigorously until the outside of the shaker is frosted and beaded with sweat.

Strain into the glasses, top each glass with a mint leaf and a lime wedge, and serve.

STRAIGHT UP

Orgeat syrup is made from almonds and sugar. Very sweet, with a strong almond flavor, orgeat syrup enhances many cocktails, most famously the mai tai. It is sometimes called almond syrup and is available online through sites that carry syrups (see Resources, page 105).

BANANA RUM FRAPPÉ

MAKES FIFTEEN 5½-OUNCE DRINKS

Even if you're sure you don't need to make the full fifteen servings this recipe allows for, go ahead and make the full recipe of banana rum. It has a number of good uses (see Bonus from the Bar) and keeps indefinitely once the bananas are strained.

FOR THE BANANA RUM

12 DRIED BANANA SLICES OR 2 CUPS DRIED BANANA CHIPS

4 OUNCES BOILING WATER

2 OUNCES UNSULFURED MOLASSES

¼ CUP PACKED BROWN SUGAR

1 LITER DARK RUM

1 LARGE VANILLA BEAN

FOR THE COCKTAIL

4 TABLESPOONS GRANULATED SUGAR FOR RIMMING THE GLASSES

4 TABLESPOONS SHREDDED COCONUT, TOASTED, FOR RIMMING THE GLASSES, PLUS MORE FOR GARNISH

1 LEMON OR LIME WEDGE FOR RIMMING THE GLASSES

16 OUNCES PINEAPPLE JUICE

CRUSHED ICE FOR SERVING

DRIED PINEAPPLE SLICES OR BANANA CHIPS FOR GARNISH

GLASSWARE

15 MARGARITA COUPES OR LARGE MARTINI GLASSES

PLANNING AHEAD

The banana rum can be made as few as 4 hours in advance, but it is ideal after 48 hours.

To prepare the banana rum, cut the dried banana slices in half and place them in a large canning jar or pitcher with a tight-fitting lid. Add the water, molasses, and brown sugar, stir well, and let sit for 2 minutes.

Stir in the rum. Split the vanilla bean in half lengthwise and scrape out the seeds. Add the seeds and bean to the rum. Shake or stir vigorously to mix all the ingredients. Refrigerate for up to 48 hours, stirring or shaking occasionally. After 48 hours at most, strain the rum, discarding the vanilla bean and reserving the bananas for another use (see Bonus from the Bar).

When ready to serve, pour the granulated sugar and coconut into a small bowl and mix together thoroughly. Transfer the coconut sugar to a small plate. Rub the juicy side of the lemon or lime wedge along the outer edge of the lip of each coupe—not along the inside of the rim. Holding each coupe at an angle, roll the outer edge of the rim in the sugar until it is fully coated.

Fill a large pitcher with ice, add the banana rum and pineapple juice, and stir briskly until the pitcher is beaded with sweat and frosty.

Place crushed ice in the prepared coupes. Pour the frappé over the ice, garnish with dried pineapple slices or banana chips, sprinkle with coconut, and serve.

VARIATION

Banana Rum Punch: Peel and freeze 4 large, ripe, fresh bananas until firm. Place them in a punch bowl and add the banana rum with the dried bananas, pineapple juice, and 1 liter pear or apple cider or 1 liter ginger beer. Sprinkle shredded coconut over the top and serve.

✳ BONUS FROM THE BAR
The bananas that are strained out of the banana rum make a delicious topping for ice cream or cake. Also, once the pineapple juice is added, the cocktail mix itself (combined with some soy sauce) can be used as a marinade and base for grilled chicken or fish.

SUMMER SUNSET

In this drink, the richness of the rum and port is balanced by the acidity of the lemon juice. Serve this before a summer barbecue or even after the main meal.

ICE FOR SERVING

16 OUNCES LEMON SOUR MIX (PAGE 22)

8 OUNCES DARK RUM

4 OUNCES RUBY PORT

FOUR 1/8-INCH-THICK ROUND ORANGE SLICES FOR GARNISH

4 OUNCES CHERRY BRANDY

GLASSWARE

4 ROCKS GLASSES

Fill the rocks glasses with ice.

Fill a large pitcher with ice and add the sour mix, rum, and port. Stir briskly until the mixture is frothy and the pitcher is beaded with sweat and frosty.

Strain the rum mixture into the glasses and lay an orange slice on top of each drink.

Gently pour 1 ounce cherry brandy over each orange slice and serve just before sunset.

COCONUT RUM FRAPPÉ

MAKES FOUR 3-OUNCE DRINKS

This frappé starts out tasting like a daiquiri and ends up tasting like a piña colada. Use dark (but not heavy) rum, such as Mount Gay, which is medium weight with great caramel flavor and a good kick.

I PINT COCONUT SORBET

I LIME

2 TABLESPOONS SHREDDED COCONUT FOR RIMMING THE GLASSES

2 TEASPOONS SUGAR

8 OUNCES DARK RUM

CRUSHED ICE FOR SERVING

GLASSWARE

4 OLD-FASHIONED GLASSES

PLANNING AHEAD
The sorbet ice cubes should be made at least 1 hour before serving and can be made up to a week in advance and stored in the freezer.

To prepare the sorbet ice cubes, let the sorbet soften at room temperature for 15 minutes or microwave it for 30 seconds. Spread the sorbet in an ice cube tray and freeze until solid, at least 1 hour.

When ready to serve, cut the lime into 8 wedges. Pour the coconut onto a small plate. Rub the juicy side of a lime wedge along the outer edge of the lip of each old-fashioned glass—not along the inside of the rim. Holding each glass at an angle, roll the outer edge of the rim in the coconut until it is fully coated.

Place 2 lime wedges and ½ teaspoon sugar in each glass. Muddle the limes (see page 11) to extract the juice. Evenly divide the rum among the glasses and stir.

Add the coconut sorbet ice cubes and enough crushed ice to fill each glass and serve.

WATERMELON COOLER

After a day at the beach, there's nothing better to sip while you are waiting for the hot dogs to grill. For a punch version of this recipe, see Watermelon Punch (page 64). Use seedless watermelon if available; if not, remove the seeds or just ignore them.

½ SMALL WATERMELON

8 OUNCES SIMPLE SYRUP (PAGE 17)

4 OUNCES FRESH LEMON JUICE
(FROM APPROXIMATELY 3 LEMONS)

4 OUNCES FRESH LIME JUICE
(FROM APPROXIMATELY 4 LIMES)

ICE FOR SERVING

12 OUNCES DARK RUM

8 OUNCES VANILLA LIQUEUR

12 FRESH MINT LEAVES FOR GARNISH

GLASSWARE

4 COOLER GLASSES OR ANY
OTHER LARGE GLASSES

PLANNING AHEAD
The watermelon must be frozen for at least 30 minutes.

To prepare the watermelon, cut off the rind and discard. Cut the flesh into 1-inch cubes (you should have about 4 cups) and place them in a colander set inside a bowl. Stir the cubes gently to extract as much juice as possible. The more you stir, the more juice will be extruded; just be careful not to overdo it and break down the melon. You should have at least 8 ounces of juice. Set the watermelon juice aside.

Place the watermelon cubes in a freezer bag and freeze for at least 30 minutes.

Mix the syrup, lemon juice, and lime juice with the extracted watermelon juice.

(continued)

When ready to serve, divide the frozen watermelon among the cooler glasses. Add ice cubes to top off each glass. Evenly divide the rum, vanilla liqueur, and watermelon juice mixture among the glasses and stir thoroughly. Don't worry if the watermelon breaks down a bit—this adds flavor to the drink. Garnish with mint leaves and serve.

FROZEN MANGO SMASH

The creamy texture of mangoes makes them perfect for frozen drinks.
Overripe fruit works especially well in this recipe.

1 RIPE MANGO

8 OUNCES WHITE RUM

3 OUNCES TRIPLE SEC

3 OUNCES APRICOT BRANDY

6 OUNCES FRESH LIME JUICE (FROM
APPROXIMATELY 6 LIMES)

CRUSHED ICE FOR SERVING

GLASSWARE

4 HURRICANE GLASSES OR
ANY OTHER LARGE GLASSES

Carefully peel the mango and
cut the flesh into 1-inch cubes,
discarding the pit. Scrape the
remaining fruit off the skin of the
mango and add it to the cubes.
Cut the longest strips of skin into
4 long strips for garnish and set
aside.

In a large pitcher, combine the
rum, triple sec, apricot brandy,
and lime juice.

Process in a blender in two
batches, using half the mango,
half the rum mixture, and 1 cup
crushed ice per batch. Blend until
smooth.

Pour into the hurricane glasses,
garnish each with a strip of mango
peel, and serve.

LAVA FLOW

Frozen drinks are better served in the late afternoon rather than right before dinner, when they tend to fill you up. This drink is a flowing version of the Piña Colada (page 51).

12 OUNCES PINEAPPLE JUICE

12 OUNCES COCONUT RUM

12 OUNCES WHITE RUM

6 OUNCES COCONUT MILK

6 OUNCES COCO LOPEZ CREAM OF COCONUT

4 CUPS CRUSHED ICE

4 OUNCES GRENADINE, HOMEMADE (SEE PAGE 45) OR STORE-BOUGHT

GLASSWARE

4 HURRICANE GLASSES OR ANY OTHER LARGE GLASSES

PLANNING AHEAD
The base can be made up to 8 hours in advance and stored in the refrigerator.

In a large pitcher, combine the pineapple juice, both rums, the milk, and the cream of coconut.

Process in a blender in two batches, using 24 ounces mix and 2 cups crushed ice per batch.

Blend until smooth.

Pour into the hurricane glasses. Float 1 ounce grenadine on each and watch the lava flow.

WATERMELON PUNCH

This refreshing and fun summer cocktail is the perfect accompaniment to a homemade Mexican meal of chicken quesadillas or steak fajitas. Use seedless watermelon if available; if not, you can remove the seeds or just ignore them.

½ SMALL WATERMELON

2 LARGE BUNCHES OF FRESH MINT

1½ CUPS CONFECTIONERS' OR SUPERFINE SUGAR

1 LITER WHITE RUM

16 OUNCES WHITE GRAPE JUICE

8 OUNCES VANILLA LIQUEUR

18 OUNCES FRESH LEMON JUICE (FROM APPROXIMATELY 12 LEMONS), SOME RINDS RESERVED FOR RIMMING THE GLASSES

2 TABLESPOONS CHIPOTLE POWDER OR SMOKED PAPRIKA FOR RIMMING THE GLASSES (OPTIONAL)

1 TABLESPOON GRANULATED SUGAR FOR RIMMING THE GLASSES (OPTIONAL)

1 TABLESPOON KOSHER SALT FOR RIMMING THE GLASSES (OPTIONAL)

GLASSWARE

PUNCH CUPS
AND PUNCH BOWL

PLANNING AHEAD
The watermelon cubes will need to be frozen at least 45 minutes before serving the punch. The watermelon base requires at least 1 hour chilling time, but it is really best if left to chill overnight. It can be made up to 1 day in advance and stored in the refrigerator.

Cut the watermelon flesh into ½-inch cubes, discarding the rind. Place one-quarter of the watermelon cubes in a freezer bag and freeze until ready to use. Place the remaining melon in the punch bowl.

Tear the mint leaves off the stems. Place the leaves in a bowl and cover with cold water. Swish the leaves around once or twice, and when the water settles, transfer the leaves to a paper towel. Pat dry. Set aside half of the leaves and add the remaining leaves to the watermelon in the punch bowl.

Add the confectioners' sugar to the punch bowl. Stir the melon cubes to extract as much of the juice as possible.

Stir in the rum, white grape juice, vanilla liqueur, and lemon juice. Let chill in the refrigerator for at least 1 hour and up to 1 day (longer is better).

When ready to serve, you may rim the punch cups, if desired: On a small plate, combine the chipotle powder with the granulated sugar and salt. Rub the juicy side of the reserved lemon rind along the outer edge of the lip of each cup—not along the inside of the rim. Holding each cup at an angle, roll the outer edge of the rim in the spice mix until it is fully coated.

To serve, place a few cubes of frozen watermelon in each punch cup. Ladle in the punch and garnish with mint.

-4-

VODKA

VODKA IS A rectified spirit (distilled three times) produced from grain or potatoes. Ninety percent of the vodka produced is grain based. Occasionally, and mainly in Europe, rice or molasses is used. Though colorless and odorless, vodka has a subtle taste. Potato-based vodkas, such as Luksusowa from Poland, have very distinctive flavors. Some vodkas are distinguished by their texture, which ranges from oily to watery.

BARBECUE COCKTAIL

The Barbecue Cocktail balances the heat of jalapeños with vermouth and tomato juice to produce intriguing and complex flavors. Serve this any time a little heat is desired. It is a perfect aperitif before any grilled entrée and is a nice accompaniment to guacamole.

1 TEASPOON SMOKED PAPRIKA FOR RIMMING THE GLASSES

½ TEASPOON KOSHER SALT FOR RIMMING THE GLASSES

½ TEASPOON SUGAR FOR RIMMING THE GLASSES

1 LIME

4 OUNCES JALAPEÑO VODKA (RECIPE FOLLOWS)

1 OUNCE DRY VERMOUTH

1 OUNCE TOMATO JUICE

GLASSWARE

2 OLD-FASHIONED GLASSES

Mix the paprika, salt, and sugar on a small plate. Cut twists (see page 72) from the lime for garnish, then halve the lime crosswise. Rub the juicy side of the lime along the outer edge of the lip of each cocktail glass—not along the inside of the rim. Holding each glass at an angle, roll the outer edge of the rim in the paprika until it is fully coated.

Fill a cocktail pitcher with ice. Squeeze the juice from the lime into the pitcher. Add the jalapeño vodka, vermouth, tomato juice, and any remaining paprika mixture. Stir vigorously until the outside of the pitcher is beaded with sweat and frosty.

Strain into the prepared glasses, garnish with lime twists, and serve.

(continued)

JALAPEÑO VODKA

Not only does this vodka taste great, but it also wakes you up, clears your sinuses, and stimulates your thoughts! You can use it as a replacement for straight vodka in a martini or to make the spiciest Bloody Mary around.

6 FRESH JALAPEÑO PEPPERS

1 TEASPOON BLACK PEPPERCORNS

½ TEASPOON WHOLE ALLSPICE BERRIES (OPTIONAL)

½ TEASPOON WHOLE JUNIPER BERRIES (OPTIONAL)

1 LITER VODKA

PLANNING AHEAD
The infusion requires at least a few hours but is really best after 2 days. It can be made several weeks in advance and stored in the refrigerator.

Beginning at the pointy end, cut a slit halfway up each jalapeño pepper. Set aside.

Preheat a small nonstick pan on high heat. Add the peppercorns, and the allspice berries and juniper berries, if desired, and cook for 30 seconds. Immediately toss into a large pitcher with a tight-fitting lid.

Return the pan to the heat and add the jalapeños. Cook them until all sides are slightly toasted and blistered, about 30 seconds per side. Immediately add them to the pitcher.

Pour the vodka over the peppers and spices and tightly close the pitcher. The vodka will be ready after a few hours but is best after 2 days.

Before serving the vodka, strain it to remove the jalapeños and spices. You can either discard the peppers and spices or use them immediately for cooking.

COSMOPOLITAN

No one truly knows where the überpopular cosmopolitan came from. The only thing that can be stated with any certainty is that it appeared after citrus-flavored vodkas first arrived on the market in the 1980s. If it wasn't a classic already, the women of *Sex and the City* certainly did their part to make it one in the 1990s.

3 OUNCES CITRON VODKA

2½ OUNCES TRIPLE SEC

2 OUNCES CRANBERRY JUICE

½ OUNCE FRESH LIME JUICE
(FROM APPROXIMATELY ½ LIME)

2 ORANGE TWISTS (SEE SIDEBAR)
FOR GARNISH

GLASSWARE
2 COCKTAIL GLASSES

Fill a cocktail shaker with ice and add the vodka, triple sec, cranberry juice, and lime juice. Shake vigorously until the outside of the shaker is frosted and beaded with sweat.

Strain into the cocktail glasses, garnish with orange twists, and serve.

CITRUS TWISTS

To make the twists, start by cutting off the "polar" nubs at each end of the fruit. Hold the fruit firmly in the palm of your hand. Using a vegetable peeler, start at one end and cut straight toward the other end. Carefully and steadily remove a slice of the rind. Try not to get too much of the bitter white pith.

MOSCOW MULE

The Smirnoff Vodka Company created this wonderfully simple drink in the 1940s to help promote its brand. Ginger beer is much drier and has a more pronounced ginger flavor than ginger ale. The better versions are actually brewed just like beer and are nonalcoholic.

ICE FOR SERVING

4 OUNCES SMIRNOFF VODKA

8 OUNCES GINGER BEER

GLASSWARE

2 HIGHBALL GLASSES

Fill the highball glasses with ice.

Add 2 ounces vodka and 4 ounces ginger beer to each glass. Stir well and serve.

LEMON FRAPPÉ

MAKES FOUR 5-OUNCE DRINKS

Limoncello is an Italian cordial made by macerating lemon peels in sugar and then adding grappa or another clear distillate. The mixture sits until the flavors are blended according to the house style. It is relatively easy to find. Knapp Winery in New York's Finger Lakes wine region makes an excellent domestic version, or you can easily make your own.

CRUSHED ICE FOR SERVING

1 LEMON, QUARTERED

1 ORANGE OR LIME

8 OUNCES VODKA OR GIN

8 OUNCES LIMONCELLO, HOMEMADE
(SEE PAGE 29) OR STORE-BOUGHT

GLASSWARE

4 WINEGLASSES

Fill each wineglass with crushed ice. Squeeze a lemon wedge into each glass, then drop the lemon in. Using a zester, cut long strands from the orange or lime and lay them on top of the ice.

Pour 2 ounces each of the vodka or gin and limoncello into the glasses, stir until well blended, and serve.

SALTY DOG

Try using Hawaiian Alaea sea salt to rim the glass for this drink. Mixed with powdered Hawaiian red clay, the salt's brick-orange color and robust salinity beautifully complement the rosy hue and refreshingly tart and citrusy flavor of the Salty Dog.

I TO 1½ GRAPEFRUITS

2 TABLESPOONS HAWAIIAN ALAEA SEA SALT (SEE RESOURCES, PAGE 105) OR KOSHER SALT FOR RIMMING GLASSES

8 OUNCES VODKA OR GIN

2 OUNCES SWEET VERMOUTH

2 OUNCES COINTREAU

GLASSWARE

4 COCKTAIL GLASSES

Remove four long strips (twists) of rind from the grapefruit, being careful not to remove very much of the white pith (see page 72). Cut the grapefruit in half and squeeze the juice from each half (you should have about 8 ounces) and set aside. Reserve one grapefruit rind.

Pour the salt onto a small plate. Cut the reserved grapefruit rind in half, then rub the juicy side of the fruit along the outer edge of the lip of each cocktail glass—not along the inside of the rim. Holding each glass at an angle, roll the outer edge of the rim in the salt until it is fully coated.

Fill a cocktail shaker with ice and add the vodka, vermouth, Cointreau, and grapefruit juice. Shake vigorously until the outside of the shaker is thoroughly beaded with sweat and is extremely cold to the touch.

Strain into the prepared glasses, add a grapefruit twist to each, and serve.

CHAPTER

-5-

WINE & SPARKLING WINE

WHEN MAKING DRINKS based on still wines, there are three simple rules that apply to both red and white wine. First, use a wine that you would like to drink on its own. Second, use wines that are fruit-forward, meaning they taste either unctuous and "grapey" or similar to other fruits and berries. Third, use wines that have crisp, bracing acidity. The acidity brings freshness and liveliness to the resulting beverage.

WHILE MOST PEOPLE think about serving sparkling wines for a special occasion, they are actually great food wines, perfect for brunch, lunch, or a dinner party. Their acidity and effervescence cut through rich foods and are a refreshing counterbalance to hot, spicy dishes. They also make interesting, decadent cocktails.

UNLESS OTHERWISE SPECIFIED, all the recipes in this chapter use a brut-style sparkling wine. Brut is one of the driest styles of sparkling wines and also the most widely available. All Champagnes are sparkling wines; not all sparkling wines, however, are Champagnes. Champagne is made only in the Champagne region of France, about sixty miles east of Paris. Any sparkling wine that does not come from this region is not true Champagne.

CLASSIC SANGRIA

MAKES TEN 5-OUNCE SERVINGS

Sangria was originally developed as a quick way to hide the flaws in weak, acidic, or simply poor wine. Since well-made wine is so abundant today, we do not need to drink sangria out of necessity; rather, we drink it for the taste. Sangria makes a great aperitif, is always welcome at a barbecue, and jazzes up any Sunday brunch.

I LEMON, SLICED INTO ½-INCH-THICK ROUNDS

I LIME, SLICED INTO ½-INCH-THICK ROUNDS

2 ORANGES, SLICED INTO ½-INCH-THICK ROUNDS

½ CUP SUGAR

8 OUNCES TRIPLE SEC, CHILLED

8 OUNCES BRANDY, CHILLED

8 OUNCES FRESH ORANGE JUICE (FROM 2 TO 3 ORANGES), CHILLED

ONE 750-MILLILITER BOTTLE DRY RED WINE, CHILLED

GLASSWARE

WINEGLASSES AND LARGE PITCHER OR PUNCH BOWL

PLANNING AHEAD
Chill all the ingredients and the pitcher or punch bowl for at least 30 minutes before preparing the sangria.

Place the fruit in the pitcher or punch bowl. Sprinkle the sugar on top and muddle the fruit (see page 11) to extract some of the juice.

Add the triple sec and brandy and stir well to dissolve the sugar.

Add the orange juice and wine. Let stand for 5 minutes before serving.

PEACH SANGRIA

Use a white wine with good fruit and acidity, such as a Riesling, or rosé in this recipe.

4 PEACHES

6 WHOLE PIECES OF STAR ANISE

6 CARDAMOM PODS

I CINNAMON STICK

I VANILLA BEAN, SPLIT IN HALF
LENGTHWISE

8 OUNCES BOILING WATER

½ CUP SUPERFINE SUGAR

4 OUNCES FRESH ORANGE JUICE
(FROM I TO 2 ORANGES)

3 OUNCES FRESH LEMON JUICE
(FROM 2 LEMONS)

2 OUNCES FRESH LIME JUICE
(FROM 2 LIMES)

TWO 750-MILLILITER BOTTLES WHITE
WINE, CHILLED

16 OUNCES PEACH EAU-DE-VIE (SEE
STRAIGHT UP) OR PEACH BRANDY,
CHILLED

16 OUNCES PEACH NECTAR, CHILLED

ICE CUBES FOR SERVING

MINT LEAVES FOR GARNISH

GLASSWARE

WINEGLASSES AND
LARGE PITCHER OR
PUNCH BOWL

PLANNING AHEAD
The base requires up to 1 hour in the
refrigerator. Chill the wine, brandy,
and peach nectar for at least 30
minutes before preparing the sangria.

To prepare the peaches, bring a large pot of water to a boil and have ready a large bowl of ice-cold water. Score the bottom of each peach with a tiny X and place it in the boiling water. Remove after 30 seconds and plunge into the cold water. Starting at the scored bottom, use a paring knife to help pull the skin off each peach. If it is too difficult, return the peach to the boiling water for a few seconds.

(continued)

Cut the peeled peaches into eighths, discarding the pit.

Place the star anise, cardamom, cinnamon stick, and vanilla bean in the punch bowl and pour the 8 ounces boiling water over them. Add the sugar and stir until it has fully dissolved. Add the peaches and citrus juices and let the mixture steep in the refrigerator for up to one hour (the longer it steeps, the more the peach flavor will develop).

When ready to serve, add the wine, eau-de-vie, nectar , and ice and stir until well blended. Float several mint leaves on top of the punch and serve.

STRAIGHT UP

Eau-de-vie is clear, unaged brandy produced by distilling wine made from grapes or other fruit. Eaux-de-vie are often called by the French word for whatever fruit they are made from, thus pêche is peach eau-de-vie and framboise is raspberry eau-de-vie. (When made from grapes, eau-de-vie is known as grappa in Italy, and a lightly aged version made in Burgundy is called marc.) Used as mixers, eaux-de-vie add fruit flavor without any syrupiness, so they make an interesting substitution for brandy in mixed drinks.

STRAWBERRY KIWI SANGRIA

Crème de fraise is a strawberry liqueur. It is generally easy to find, but if you have trouble, you can substitute strawberry schnapps or another berry cordial.

1 PINT STRAWBERRIES, CLEANED, HULLED, AND HALVED

3 KIWIFRUITS, PEELED AND SLICED INTO ½-INCH-THICK ROUNDS

¼ CUP SUGAR

ONE 750-MILLILITER BOTTLE FRUITY ROSÉ WINE, CHILLED

8 OUNCES CRÈME DE FRAISE OR STRAWBERRY SCHNAPPS OR ANOTHER BERRY CORDIAL, CHILLED

8 OUNCES WHITE RUM, CHILLED

8 OUNCES WHITE GRAPE JUICE, CHILLED

GLASSWARE

WINEGLASSES AND LARGE PITCHER OR PUNCH BOWL

PLANNING AHEAD
Chill all the ingredients and the pitcher or punch bowl for at least 30 minutes before preparing the sangria.

Place the fruit in the pitcher or punch bowl and stir in the sugar. Let stand for 5 minutes to extract the juices.

Stir in the wine, crème de fraise, rum, and grape juice and let stand for 5 minutes before serving.

CHAMPAGNE SANGRIA

Very ripe red plums add both flavor and color to this sparkling play on a classic sangria.

4 PLUMS, PITTED AND CUT INTO THICK WEDGES

½ CUP SUPERFINE OR CONFECTIONERS' SUGAR

32 OUNCES APRICOT NECTAR OR PEACH, PEAR, OR OTHER NECTAR, CHILLED

16 OUNCES PLUM WINE, CHILLED

8 OUNCES BRANDY, CHILLED

TWO 750-MILLILITER BOTTLES SPARKLING WINE, CHILLED

MINT LEAVES FOR GARNISH

GLASSWARE

PUNCH CUPS

AND PUNCH BOWL

PLANNING AHEAD
Chill all the ingredients for at least 30 minutes before preparing the sangria.

Place the plums and sugar in the punch bowl and stir well to extract the juice. Add the nectar, plum wine, and brandy. Stir well and refrigerate until ready to serve.

To serve, remove the mixture from the refrigerator. Add the sparkling wine and stir briefly to combine. Float mint leaves on top and serve immediately.

MOSCATO COOLER

MAKES FIVE 7-OUNCE DRINKS

Slightly sweet, low-alcohol Moscato is a sparkling counterpoint to the orange juice and Cointreau in this version of the Magnificent Mimosa (page 87), adapted for slow drinking on summer afternoons.

1 TABLESPOON SUGAR FOR RIMMING THE GLASSES

1 TABLESPOON GRATED ORANGE ZEST, FLESH RESERVED FOR RIMMING THE GLASSES

ICE FOR SERVING

5 OUNCES COINTREAU

5 OUNCES FRESH ORANGE JUICE (FROM APPROXIMATELY 2 ORANGES)

ONE 750-MILLILITER BOTTLE SPARKLING MOSCATO, CHILLED

GLASSWARE
5 WINEGLASSES

PLANNING AHEAD
Chill the Moscato for at least 30 minutes before preparing the coolers.

Mix the sugar and orange zest on a small plate. Cut a wedge from the reserved orange. Rub the juicy side of the orange wedge along the outer edge of the lip of each wineglass—not along the inside of the rim. Holding each glass at an angle, roll the outer edge of the rim in the sugar until it is fully coated.

Fill the wineglasses with ice.

Add 1 ounce Cointreau and 1 ounce orange juice to each glass.

Fill with Moscato, stir gently, and serve.

MAGNIFICENT MIMOSA

MAKES SIX 6-OUNCE DRINKS

The mimosa gets a bum rap and is too often served as a cheap add-on during a price-fixed brunch. These concoctions of not-so-great Champagne and too much orange juice have tarnished the image of the mimosa. Using fresh-squeezed juice and Cointreau will give you a delightful beverage worthy of your dinner table. The mimosa makes a wonderful aperitif, or try serving it with a first course of smoked salmon or seared scallops. And unlike most still, dry wines, the mimosa will stand up to a strong vinaigrette in a salad course.

ONE 750-MILLILITER BOTTLE SPARKLING WINE, CHILLED

12 OUNCES FRESH ORANGE JUICE (FROM APPROXIMATELY 4 ORANGES)

3 OUNCES COINTREAU

GLASSWARE

6 CHAMPAGNE GLASSES

PLANNING AHEAD
Chill the sparkling wine for at least 30 minutes before making the cocktails.

Divide the sparkling wine among the Champagne glasses. This will work out to approximately 4 ounces per glass.

Top each glass with 2 ounces orange juice, then float ½ ounce Cointreau on top of each and serve. Sip slowly.

GINGER CHAMPAGNE PUNCH

MAKES EIGHTEEN 4-OUNCE OR TWELVE 6-OUNCE SERVINGS

The tangy sweetness of ginger, lime, and sparkling wine makes this cocktail a wonderful palate opener before dinner or a soothing restorative after. Or serve it with food—it's especially good with Asian dishes.

16 OUNCES GINGER SYRUP (PAGE 18), CHILLED

8 OUNCES FRESH LIME JUICE (FROM APPROXIMATELY 8 LIMES), CHILLED

TWO 750-MILLILITER BOTTLES SPARKLING WINE, CHILLED

1 LIME, CUT INTO 8 THIN SLICES

GLASSWARE

PUNCH CUPS OR CHAMPAGNE GLASSES AND PUNCH BOWL

Place the ginger syrup and lime juice in the punch bowl. Stir well to blend.

Add the sparkling wine and mix gently but thoroughly.

Float the lime slices on top and serve.

TRICK OF THE TRADE
If you are serving this punch in Champagne glasses (or collins glasses, as shown here), you can rim the glasses (see page 11) with a mixture of equal parts powdered ginger and granulated sugar.

PLANNING AHEAD
The punch should be served very cold, so either refrigerate all the ingredients the night before you assemble the punch, or chill the prepared punch overnight.

NONALCOHOLIC

DRINKS

AT ANY GIVEN party, you will likely host at least one person who is not drinking alcohol for one reason or another. However, sugary sodas don't whet the appetite and rarely make a good accompaniment to the food being served. Nonalcoholic beer can be quite good, but at times something less filling and more interesting is called for. It's also nice to offer something for kids.

WITH THAT IN mind, this chapter has traditional favorites, such as a variety of lemonades (pages 94 to 96), and alcohol-free cocktails, such as the Summer Solstice (page 99) and the Faux Margarita (page 101). These should satisfy the most discerning nonalcoholic-beverage consumer. Many are ideal summertime drinks, so refreshing that the missing alcohol is unlikely to be noticed by even the most die-hard fans of hard drinks.

AND DON'T FORGET that any one of these "cocktails" can be made alcoholic by simply adding a splash of your favorite liquor. So if you're trying to please a diverse group and you have only enough space or time for one drink, consider making one of the delicious selections from this chapter and arranging bottles of a few base liquors—rum, vodka, and gin would be a fine start—so guests can spike their own.

ICED TEA

A summertime favorite, this iced tea can be mixed with lemonade or limeade, Southern Comfort, or Limoncello (page 29). It can be steeped with cinnamon, clove, or star anise for warm undertones. For a richer flavor, you can sweeten it with Mint Syrup or Berry Syrup (page 18).

12 TEA BAGS

1 LEMON OR ORANGE

64 OUNCES BOILING WATER

ICE FOR SERVING

SIMPLE SYRUP (PAGE 17) FOR SERVING
(OPTIONAL)

GLASSWARE

8 ICED-TEA GLASSES

PLANNING AHEAD
The iced tea can be made up to
8 hours in advance and stored in the
refrigerator.

Place the tea bags in a large glass pitcher.

Peel the lemon or orange. Cut the peel into very large pieces and add them to the pitcher.

Pour the boiling water into the pitcher and let steep for at least 10 minutes.

Remove the tea bags and discard. Refrigerate the tea until cool.

To serve, fill the glasses with ice and add the tea. Sweeten, if desired, with simple syrup.

LEMONADE

Fresh lemonade does not have to be syrupy sweet. The sweetness level and body are up to you: For lighter body, add more water; for more sweetness, add more syrup.

32 OUNCES FRESH LEMON JUICE
(FROM 24 TO 30 LEMONS)

8 TO 16 OUNCES SIMPLE SYRUP (PAGE 17),
VANILLA SYRUP (PAGE 18), OR PINEAPPLE
SYRUP (PAGE 18)

8 TO 16 OUNCES ICE WATER

ICE FOR SERVING

8 MINT LEAVES FOR GARNISH

GLASSWARE

ICED-TEA OR
COOLER GLASSES

PLANNING AHEAD
The lemonade can be made up to
8 hours in advance and stored in the
refrigerator.

Place the lemon juice and 8 ounces each of syrup and ice water in a large pitcher. Stir well.

Taste and add more water or syrup, if necessary. Serve over ice with a mint leaf in each glass.

WATERMELON LEMONADE

This recipe combines two summer favorites: watermelon and fresh lemonade. If the melon yields a great deal of juice, you will not need to add water. If the melon is less juicy or less ripe, you may need to add more. Taste the lemonade before serving and adjust as needed.

1 SMALL WATERMELON (10 POUNDS OR LESS)

¼ CUP SUGAR

32 OUNCES FRESH LEMON JUICE (FROM 24 TO 30 LEMONS)

8 TO 16 OUNCES SIMPLE SYRUP (PAGE 17)

UP TO 16 OUNCES ICE WATER

ICE FOR SERVING

GLASSWARE

ICED-TEA OR COOLER GLASSES

PLANNING AHEAD
The lemonade can be made up to 8 hours in advance and stored in the refrigerator.

Cut the watermelon into 2-inch cubes. Place the cubes in a colander set inside a bowl and sprinkle with sugar. Stir the watermelon to exude the juice. You will get anywhere from 8 to 24 ounces of juice, depending on the ripeness of the melon. Reserve the leftover melon for another use.

Pour the lemon juice and the watermelon juice into a large pitcher. Add 8 ounces syrup and stir well.

Taste and add ice water or more syrup if necessary. Serve over ice.

BLUEBERRY LEMONADE

Here, blueberries mellow the high acidity of the lemonade, making it more food friendly. This drink is the perfect refresher for summertime barbecues.

1 CUP FRESH BLUEBERRIES

2 TABLESPOONS SUGAR

32 OUNCES FRESH LEMON JUICE
(FROM 24 TO 30 LEMONS)

8 TO 16 OUNCES SIMPLE SYRUP (PAGE 17)

8 TO 16 OUNCES ICE WATER

ICE FOR SERVING

GLASSWARE

ICED-TEA OR
COOLER GLASSES

PLANNING AHEAD
*The lemonade can be made up to
8 hours in advance and stored in the
refrigerator.*

Place the blueberries in a large pitcher and sprinkle with the sugar. Use a wooden spoon to mash about half the blueberries against the sides of the pitcher to extract their juice.

Stir the lemon juice into the blueberries.

Add 8 ounces each of syrup and ice water and stir well.

Taste and add more syrup or water if necessary. Serve over ice.

LIMEADE

Limes are often sweeter than lemons, so definitely taste the limeade as you make it. You might need less syrup than you would were you making an equal amount of lemonade.

32 OUNCES FRESH LIME JUICE
(FROM 24 TO 30 LIMES)

8 TO 16 OUNCES SIMPLE SYRUP (PAGE 17),
VANILLA SYRUP (PAGE 18), MINT SYRUP
(PAGE 18), OR PINEAPPLE SYRUP (PAGE 18)

8 TO 16 OUNCES ICE WATER

ICE FOR SERVING

GLASSWARE

ICED-TEA OR
COOLER GLASSES

> **PLANNING AHEAD**
> *The limeade can be made up to 8 hours in advance and stored in the refrigerator.*

Place the lime juice and 8 ounces each of simple syrup and ice water in a large pitcher. Stir well.

Taste and add more syrup or water if necessary. Serve over ice.

VARIATIONS

Coconut Limeade: Add two 10-ounce cans unsweetened coconut milk to the lime juice and water and use 8 to 16 ounces Simple Syrup (page 17) or Pineapple Syrup (page 18).

Mango Limeade: Place 1 large ripe mango, peeled and diced into 1-inch cubes, in a large pitcher and toss with 2 tablespoons sugar. Stir well with a wooden spoon, mashing some of the mango against the sides of the pitcher to extract the juice. Add the mixture to the lime juice, syrup, and water.

SUMMER SOLSTICE

This nonalcoholic drink is the closest thing you'll find to an alcohol-based cocktail. Verjus, the juice of unripe grapes, lends a delicate flavor and a hint of sweetness.

3 OUNCES FRESH LEMON JUICE
(FROM APPROXIMATELY 2 LEMONS)

12 OUNCES VERJUS

8 DASHES ORANGE BITTERS

8 RED GRAPES FOR GARNISH

GLASSWARE
4 COCKTAIL GLASSES

Fill a cocktail shaker with ice and add the lemon juice, verjus, and bitters.

Shake vigorously until the outside of the shaker is frosted and beaded with sweat.

Strain into the cocktail glasses and garnish each with 2 grapes speared on toothpicks.

FAUX MOJITO

The mojito is one of the world's great cocktails, even without the rum.

2 LIMES, CUT INTO EIGHTHS

4 TEASPOONS SUGAR

12 MINT LEAVES

ICE FOR SERVING

20 OUNCES CLUB SODA

GLASSWARE

4 ROCKS GLASSES

Place 4 pieces of lime in each rocks glass.

Add 1 teaspoon sugar and 3 mint leaves to each glass. Muddle together (see page 11).

Fill the glasses with ice, top with club soda, and serve.

FAUX MARGARITA

This cocktail is more savory than sweet. Orange flower water is very potent, so be careful not to use more than what is called for.

4 LIMES

4 TEASPOONS SUGAR

8 DASHES ORANGE BITTERS

2 TEASPOONS ORANGE FLOWER WATER

KOSHER SALT FOR RIMMING THE GLASSES

ICE FOR SERVING

24 OUNCES SLIGHTLY SPARKLING MINERAL WATER, VERY COLD

GLASSWARE

4 HIGHBALL GLASSES

Using a zester, cut long pieces of zest from the limes and set aside. Cut off and discard all the white pith and any remaining zest from the limes, then cut the fruit into quarters and transfer all the pieces except one to a bowl.

Sprinkle the sugar over the limes and add the orange bitters and orange flower water. Muddle very well (see page 11).

Pour the salt onto a small plate. Rub the reserved piece of lime along the outer edge of the lip of each highball glass—not along the inside of the rim. Holding each glass at an angle, roll the outer edge of the rim in the salt until it is fully coated.

Fill each glass halfway with ice. Divide the lime mixture among the glasses. Fill the rest of the way with ice, then top off with the mineral water. Stir well.

Float some lime zest on top of each drink and serve.

VIRGIN WATERMELON PUNCH

Here is a nonalcoholic variation of rum-spiked Watermelon Punch (page 64).

1 SMALL (10 POUNDS OR LESS) WATERMELON

16 OUNCES SIMPLE SYRUP (PAGE 17)

8 OUNCES FRESH LEMON JUICE (FROM APPROXIMATELY 6 LEMONS)

8 OUNCES FRESH LIME JUICE (FROM APPROXIMATELY 8 LIMES)

1 TEASPOON VANILLA EXTRACT

1 TEASPOON ORANGE BITTERS

½ CUP BLUEBERRIES FOR GARNISH

4 MINT SPRIGS FOR GARNISH

1 LITER GINGER ALE

GLASSWARE

PUNCH CUPS AND PUNCH BOWL

PLANNING AHEAD
The watermelon cubes must be frozen for at least 30 minutes.

To prepare the watermelon, cut the rind away from the flesh and discard. Cut the flesh into 1-inch cubes (you should have 6 to 8 cups) and place them in a colander set inside a bowl. Stir the cubes gently to extract as much juice as possible. The more you stir, the more juice will be extracted; just be careful not to overdo it and break down the melon. You should have at least 8 ounces and up to 16 ounces of juice. Set the watermelon juice aside.

Place the watermelon cubes in a freezer bag and freeze for at least 30 minutes.

(continued)

Mix the syrup, lemon juice, lime juice, vanilla extract, and orange bitters with the extracted watermelon juice. Chill the mixture while the watermelon cubes are freezing.

When ready to serve, place the watermelon cubes in the punch bowl with the blueberries and mint. Add the watermelon juice mixture and stir well. Add the ginger ale and serve.

RESOURCES

For bitters, syrups, and mixes:
Fee Brothers
800-961-FEES (800-961-3337)
feebrothers.com

For cocktail mixes and syrups:
Trader Vic's
925-675-6400
tradervics.com

For bar supplies, top to bottom:
Cocktail Kingdom
212-647-9166
cocktailkingdom.com

For a diverse selection of bar
supplies—jiggers, stirrers,
mixing glasses, you name it:
Bar Supplies
800-BLOODY-MARY
(800-256-6396)
barsupplies.com

For spices:
BulkFoods.com
419-537-1713
bulkfoods.com

For spices and dried herbs:
Penzeys Spices
800-741-7787
penzeys.com

For dried fruits, nuts, and
preserves:
American Spoon
888-735-6700
spoon.com

For a broad range of spices,
dried herbs, and flavorings,
including rose water and
orange flower water:
The Spice House
312-676-2414
thespicehouse.com

For all sorts of things, from bar supplies to paper supplies to juices:
Food Service Direct
424-373-3663
foodservicedirect.com

For lime juice and other specialties:
Nellie and Joe's
800-LIME-PIE (800-546-3743)
keylimejuice.com

For lemon juice and other specialties:
Melissa's
800-588-0151
melissas.com

For quality syrups and mixers, coffees, and specialty ingredients:
Aroma Ridge
800-JAVA-123 (800-528-2123)
aromaridge.com

For superior coffees with high-quality organics:
Kobrick Coffee Co.
201-656-6313
kobricks.com

For cacao nibs, cocoa powder, and other chocolate items:
Scharffen Berger Chocolate Maker
855-972-0511
scharffenberger.com

For caper berries and all sorts of specialty ingredients:
Scandinavian Spice
877-783-7626
scandinavianspice.com

For sea salts from all over the world:
SaltWorks
800-353-7258
seasalt.com

For glassware:
Ravenscroft Crystal
212-463-9834 (wholesale)
ravenscroftcrystal.com

INDEX

CONVERSION CHARTS

Here are rounded-off equivalents between the metric system and the traditional systems that are used in the United States to measure weight and volume.

FRACTIONS

FRACTIONS	DECIMALS
⅛	.125
¼	.25
⅓	.33
⅜	.375
½	.5
⅝	.625
⅔	.67
¾	.75
⅞	.875

WEIGHTS

US/UK	METRIC
¼ oz	7 g
½ oz	15 g
1 oz	30 g
2 oz	55 g
3 oz	85 g
4 oz	110 g
5 oz	140 g
6 oz	170 g
7 oz	200 g
8 oz (½ lb)	225 g
9 oz	250 g
10 oz	280 g
11 oz	310 g
12 oz	340 g
13 oz	370 g
14 oz	400 g
15 oz	425 g
16 oz (1 lb)	455 g

VOLUME

AMERICAN	IMPERIAL	METRIC
¼ tsp		1.25 ml
½ tsp		2.5 ml
1 tsp		5 ml
½ Tbsp (1½ tsp)		7.5 ml
1 Tbsp (3 tsp)		15 ml
¼ cup (4 Tbsp)	2 fl oz	60 ml
⅓ cup (5 Tbsp)	2½ fl oz	75 ml
½ cup (8 Tbsp)	4 fl oz	125 ml
⅔ cup (10 Tbsp)	5 fl oz	150 ml
¾ cup (12 Tbsp)	6 fl oz	175 ml
1 cup (16 Tbsp)	8 fl oz	250 ml
1¼ cups	10 fl oz	300 ml
1½ cups	12 fl oz	350 ml
2 cups (1 pint)	16 fl oz	500 ml
2½ cups	20 fl oz (1 pint)	625 ml
5 cups	40 fl oz (1 qt)	1.25 l